For the Love of Quincy

The Story of a Rescue Dog

by Linda DeFrahn
illustrations by Maria Emmighausen

*Every pet has a story to tell. Quincy let me write his
for we both felt it gives hope. To all lost pets and
pet owners, we give you this story.*

Dedicated To

Kim for his everlasting patience and forbearance,
for Janice, Quincy's first Mom and rescuer,
to Dave for all his encouragement,
and to the Small Animal Clinic of East Ryegate, VT,
for taking the time to encourage me during my
endless phone calls in those first 2 months!
Thank you!

And a big thank you to Megan Delaney for her
editing work. I had more tenses than pages,
so it was a huge job.

Printed Digitally with Non-Toxic Inks, using Wind Power

Recycled Stock

TABLE OF CONTENTS

THE SEARCH

It was a very wet summer that year. It rained every day from mid June until late August. That may be why I remember it all so well.

It was the summer my husband Kim and I decided to get another dog. A rescue dog to be exact. Our Old English Sheepdog, Murphy, had been in doggy heaven for a couple years and I felt ready to move into a new dog relationship. Murphy was that one of a kind dog you've always heard about. He was my soul mate in another species. He was such a wonderful dog that when he died, we received more sympathy cards from friends, relatives and even mere acquaintances than some people receive for humans. He had a dog soul that affected everyone; even our non-dog loving friends thought Murphy was special. But my grieving for him had softened and I was ready for another dog. Indy, our 11½-year-old Aussie Shepherd was, well, 11½. She was not going to be around forever, yet was still spry and full of energy. Indy did not know it yet, but she was going to help train the new dog we would choose to welcome into our home. We have happy and productive lives in Northern New Hampshire, and we wanted another dog to love.

Like any modern woman, when I wanted information, a product, or a dog, I surfed the web. I searched all the local shelters. They were full of beagles (*no*), black, yellow and every color lab (*no-no*), hounds (definitely *no*), Rottweilers (*maybe*) and pit bulls (*Lord no*). They, of course, had various and sundry little dogs, but my husband said *NO!* We had nothing against these breeds specifically; we just did not feel they suited our needs and lifestyle.

So I started looking further afield. And further. And further. Until I was looking at a website in Arkansas. And then I saw his picture. A beautiful dog with lots of fur and gray black coloring was looking at me from my computer screen. His eyes could barely be seen through the hair. I was in love. He was thought to be part Schnauzer-part Aussie Shepherd mix.

Now, adopting a rescue dog requires only slightly less paperwork than buying a home. This particular adoption site was run by a very thorough woman named Janice. I had to give Janice lots of references! I think she wanted to send someone north to do a site review. I was thinking she was going to ask for our last 3 years of income statements, birth certificates, passports and the like. She did a long phone interview and I could tell she was still nervous. But Janice finally relented and Quincy would be shipped north.

During that phone interview she said

things that I *now* know are code. Quincy is *reserved* (nervous), *sensitive* (anxious), *chooses his friends carefully* (scared of everything), *has only growled at one other dog in the almost 2 years while here* (so dominant that only one dog would stand up to him). I say this for all of you who may not be aware of the code.

So we set a date and that is how the whole thing started.

The Pick Up

I enlisted a strapping young male friend to
help me pick up Quincy from the rescue group.
Quincy was reported to be 60 pounds of almost
2-year-old puppy, and I wanted help if necessary
to gather the puppy into the car. The first week we
were to go, the pick up van was full and we were
rescheduled. Apparently lots of rescue dogs come
north. So, after a few more scheduling issues, it was
a Wednesday, and we were on our way.

It was pouring rain. Not a light drizzle, a
drenching rain. We had to go over 3 hours south
to the southern border of New Hampshire to the
pick up site. Clay, my friend, drove in his dog-
proofed SUV, as he has 3 lively Brittany Spaniels.
We arrived and were pleased to have a 10-minute
reprieve from the rain. An RV drove up and parked.
Folks gathered around to collect their new family
members. Children giggled and hugged puppies.
Adults marveled over their new man's best friend.
At last I gave his name to the rescue staff. They
stepped back into the RV (very clean and odor-free
by the way) and came out with my new dog. He was

stressed, but beautiful. We walked him around for a short time and gave him water. Then, the sky wanted to let loose yet more rain and Quincy jumped in the car and we set off home. At first he lay on the floor behind the driver, then on the floor behind the passenger seat, and finally he slinked up onto the back seat. He lay down facing the corner, his head facing away and hiding. He had a sense of resignation undoubtedly brought on by 3 days in a moving vehicle. He became a shadow. I sighed and turned to face the windshield and the pouring rain.

Now the caretaker at the rescue said Quincy had never been on a leash, and she had put one on him and he, "did very well." Quincy had never been in a vehicle before and look where that got him! Three days trapped in a car!

Eventually we arrived at our home. Now I should describe the setup a bit to you. Kim and I live in a 200-year-old home on a dirt road that is a dead end. We have acreage to the back and look out over fields and woods. We have a million dollar view, actually.

Again, the rain took pity on us and relented for about an hour. We hooked him to the leash and out of the car we went. And Quincy kept going and going, for the collar Janice had put on him was a wee bit too large. Quincy was free. Scared witless and no idea what to do, but out of the car and free. First things first though, and he did important doggy business. Then, away he went. And could he run! For some reason and I will never understand why, he did not then, nor has he ever, tried to run completely away. But he was scared and he ran across the road and hid in the bushes.

I was walking up and down the road looking and calling for him. Then I saw him—a look I would see many, many times in the months ahead—his curious face peering out to see what I was doing. I got myself into the thicket, thankful there were minimal thorns, and sat on what would be the first of many hard, cold, wet surfaces I would sit on to collect this dog. I looked out away from him and softly hummed his name. He came and crawled into my lap. Now I could not get up. I was on the wet mossy rock holding a 60-pound, scared dog. I am in good shape, but even I cannot dead lift 60 pounds of squirming dog. I yelled to Clay that I had Quincy, and Clay climbed into the thicket finding some thorns I had missed on my way in (and reported on each one's presence). Clay lifted the dog, we got a smaller collar and Quincy and I were attached yet again.

Now to meet Indy. We let her out of the house. She went to him and sniffed. He growled. She gave him a *fine, be that way* look and gave him space. We decided to try indoors for the rain started up again. Quincy came in and we left him attached to the leash but let him roam. He headed straight for what will be his place for the next year, a corner in the kitchen between the sink and the refrigerator. He sat there and looked petrified. But everything I had read said the first week the new dog would be skittish.

Little did we realize that Quincy, my husband Kim, and I were on an adventure that would take two years. Nor could I have ever imagined how much my life would revolve around trying to get Quincy to trust us.

But I am getting ahead of myself.

THE FIRST WEEKEND

Kim and I had made some work schedule changes so someone would always be with Quincy from pick up day, Wednesday, until we both left for work Monday. I tried to feed him the night we got him and Thursday morning. I had been told he would sit on command to get his food. Well, the dog had to be in the same room with us for that to occur! So I set up a place he could eat in an adjoining room to the kitchen. He was free to come and go as he wished. He was so nervous he would only eat a couple bites, then quickly look to see if we scary humans were safely far away, yet within view.

The first full day, Thursday, Kim was working from home. He said the dog knew where he was all day but would have nothing to do with him. The dog would not go out, take a treat, nothing.

Skittish as he was, eventually important business would need attending to. So, I attached him to a leash and off we went. He was still nervous but pleased to be outdoors. But he would not pee, he would not poop. When that poor dog finally went I think he had been over 36 hours without relieving himself. He must have peed for 2 minutes straight.

This was not for lack of us trying. It seems some nervous dogs want to do these private things, well, privately. So upon the first of many consultations with the vet's office (which deserves a medal for putting up with all my SOS's) we did not encourage pee or poop. If it looked like he was thinking about it, we turned and hummed and looked the other way. I say we, but really it was I who was doing the walking. Kim could not get within 20 feet of the dog.

On Friday, Kim left for work and I was home alone with Quincy. We headed out for a walk. I tried to ignore the dog so he would attend to important doggy business. Then I left him inside and went out back to the garden. I was, fortunately, not out there very long. I returned inside and...no dog. I quickly looked all over the house, no dog. Where in the world was he? I went outside just in time to see him trotting down the road. I yelled his name. He stopped, looked back, and then promptly continued on his way. He was not running; he was just out for a stroll. I grabbed a leash, jumped into my car and took off after him. I saw him and stopped the car behind him. I got out and said his name. He turned and trotted away. I was afraid that if I tried to pass him on the road, he would run into the woods. My choices were limited at this point. So, I drove very slowly past him and sure as shooting, he darted into the woods. *Drat.* I was convinced that this was bye-bye doggy. I stopped the car, grabbed the leash and got out. I stood there.

You must realize something at this juncture— I cannot look *at* the dog. As soon as I look *at* the dog he is freaked. I spent the first 2 weeks crawling on the floor approaching him with nonthreatening dog behavior, shoulder to shoulder. Well, this is fairly easy to do inside a house. Now outside, on the road, what to do? I walked a couple steps. Was he there? Had he run off? I saw that little, curious face peering around a maple tree, looking at me with an expression I was to learn very well, "And now what are you doing?"

I was thrilled. Quincy had not run away, yet. But I still had to catch him. So I sat down in the middle of the wet dirt road looking in the opposite direction from him and started talking to the trees. Mostly I was commenting on how happy I was that there was no one else there to observe me behaving in this manner. I did not look or sound at all mentally stable. It worked. He slowly came to me and then was right next to me. I kept chattering to the trees and leashed him up. Whew. Back up to the house. But how did Quincy get out? It seems the storm door was not latching properly and he just went right on out. We were to learn there were few doors that would contain him.

PRACTICE MAKES PERFECT

Many new experiences challenged Quincy initially. But it was sometimes the simplest that would cause the most consternation. For instance, he had never seen stairs. The first couple of nights and mornings we had to drag or carry the dog up and down the stairs. Well, on Friday I could not carry him down by myself and he could not stay up there all day after being in all night, so I put the leash on him and dragged him down. I told him he was very brave and had done a great job getting down those scary stairs. That night the dragging up was easier. Saturday morning he came down the stairs all by himself. "What a good Puppy!" I told him. Then Saturday afternoon he exhibited a behavior we were to see again and again, he practiced his new talent. Kim and I were sitting at the kitchen island having lunch. All of a sudden Quincy ran up the stairs. Then back down and peered with his little face around the corner to look at me. I, careful not to look him in the face, exclaimed, "Quincy, you did the stairs!" So for the next 10 to 15 minutes, he practiced. Up and down, up and down and occasionally looking back at me to make sure all was good.

"What is that dog doing?" Kim asked.

"Practicing. He has learned a new skill and he is practicing. Practice will make perfect, you know."

Kim said, "I think we have a crazy dog."

"Yes, maybe so, but at least he can do stairs."

Houdini Dog and Living in the Woods

It is a good thing we do not always lock our doors. Monday morning Kim and I had to return to work. We planned what to do. We would leave Quincy and Indy in the sunroom that had a tile floor. We would close the door to the kitchen and put a gate at the stairs. Well, I did that. Quincy was not impressed.

Off to work I went. I was a bit nervous all day and finally couldn't take it any longer. "I have got to go," I said. "I need to check on the dog."

I drove up the driveway and there was Quincy. *Outside*. He was not bloody from glass and I could see no damage, yet. I unlocked the door and went inside. Quincy, meanwhile, is hiding somewhere outside. I opened the door to the sunroom. *Looks OK*. I looked into the office and *My, oh my*. It looked like the Tasmanian devil had had a field day in there. A whirlwind of shredded paper, shredded wood, window trim off and chewed, pulled electric cords, and a pile of doggy poop in the middle greeted me. The electric pencil sharpener cord was frazzled; it was a wonder Quincy did not electrocute himself.

Well, I said to myself, trying to be positive, "I really did need to get in here and clean this room out." There is nothing like a dog gone crazy in a room to inspire a spring-cleaning, even if it was August. The stair gate was thrown off to the side like it was a toy in his way. Upstairs the damage was less, but Quincy had obviously been trying to get out. But, how *did* he get outside? It turns out he can

open a French door latch handle. He came here
not knowing how to get up or down stairs, yet could
open a door. Thankfully, it was not locked or he
may have really hurt himself continuing to try to get
out. Now I went to collect poor Indy since she had
a very stressful day witnessing all this crazy activity.
She looked at me as if to say, "What the heck were
you thinking?"

I went outside and tried to collect Quincy, my *Houdini dog*. He took off for the copse of trees across the road. I walked up and down the road, knowing he was in there. I went into the trees. It was starting to rain (*again*). It was very wet in the woods and I had a beautiful linen suit on. So, back inside the house I went, ran upstairs and got into more appropriate *find the dog in the rain* gear. I went back into the woods.

I sat down in the wet dirt and hummed and tried to act cool. No go. I got in the car and started driving around. I never saw him. I was distraught. Kim came home; he rode his bike around trying to look for a dog that will not even come near him. I said, "I just know he is in this patch of woods. I think I hear him rustling around." Quincy would not come out.

I put dog food on the porch and we went to bed. I got up a few times in the night, and as I entered the dining room, which is next to the porch, I heard Quincy jump up and run off. At least he had not run away. But I couldn't get to the door before he was gone. He was outside and I was inside and I was still too close! Next morning found me sitting on a cold wet rock at 5 a.m. trying to entice him. I cannot see or hear Quincy but I know he is watching me. There is nothing to be done. I left food and water out on the porch and went to work.

Everyone asks, "How is the new puppy?"

"Living in the woods."

"What?"

Everyone wants to know what happened. They are incredulous; he got out of a closed house? Affirmative. For 2 days and 2 more nights I tried to get Quincy back in. He had to be cold. I spent hours one night in the cold on the porch acting really quiet trying to get him to come back. He would have none of it. Of course it was also raining most of the time so the poor dog had to be very wet and cold. Finally, Thursday, I came home and there was a respite from the continuous rain. I got the brilliant idea of using poor Indy as bait. Carrying a leash, out we went. I sat on yet another cold wet surface for this dog.

I started playing with Indy. We were just loving and carrying on in the grass. Indy was in heaven. She made all kinds of doggy moaning happy noises. Well, Quincy could not stand it. It took no more than 5 minutes before he barreled out of the

woods, ran across the road, and through the fence to run us over. He wanted to play too! I attached him to the leash and tried playing. He realized, a minute too late, that he was close to me, a scary human, but I had him. I had no idea what I was going to do with him, but I had him.

I was to become the dog whisperer of the street. I was to learn all about dogs. I had trained my other dogs and had the basic knowledge. Now I would learn about troubled dogs. I started crawling on the floor if I wanted to get close, so as to never look Quincy in the eye. I offered his food shoulder to shoulder to him until finally he would come into the kitchen to eat. I do not think I looked the dog in the face more than twice for 8 months. If I did, he would cower and hide.

I called the vet's office. What to do? I had time over the weekend but Monday would come again. (Mondays are like that.) I could not leave him inside. He would have nothing to do with a crate, and I knew he would seriously hurt himself if I left him in it against his will. It was decided to leave Quincy outside. We were concerned if I tied him up he would hurt himself. We had tried a long running tie and that was not a happy time.

So Monday morning came. I let him out, unleashed. He stood on the porch and looked at me. I bravely looked at him and said, "Well, Quincy, it is up to you. Either you will be here when I come back or you will not. If you are still here, great. If not, good luck in your future travels."

When I drove up the driveway that evening, there he was. Waiting. Not looking at me, but waiting. And then he even came inside for dinner, wisely deciding that even scary humans were better than wet cold woods.

Whew, the end of our first 12 days and we still had a dog.

Drugs are Good

We still had a dog, but what a dog. We could
not leave him inside. We could not tie him outside.
We could not look at him. We could barely be in the
same room with him. I had to crawl on my hands
and knees and come shoulder to shoulder to him to
get close enough to give him treats. I crawled around
on the floor for 2 weeks trying to be non-threaten-
ing. I started reading everything I could find, and
watched some educational videos on dogs and dog
training. Many of these things were worthless to me,
for Quincy was so crazy and anxious that I could not
do *normal* dog training.

Even peeing and pooping was a problem.
I attached many leashes together for a very long
line. That second weekend I did not let him off
that leash for anything. So eventually, even Quincy
relented enough to pee and poop. I had to disregard
everything I knew about training dogs. It was going
to be a brand new type of training. When he peed
I ignored him. (Although privately rejoicing that
he had *finally* done the deed.) When he pooped, I
ignored him. I do not know if it was stubbornness

or shyness, but man could this puppy hold it! I was so concerned that if I caved in that weekend and let him off the leash he would be back in the woods.

Over those next 3 days we gradually developed a bit of a routine. He, like all dogs (*and many humans*) loves routine. His love of routine seemed to be the only normal thing about him those first months. He started to eat his food—although not in the kitchen yet—and not without anxiety. He was afraid to be apart from us, yet afraid to be with us. I would like to think he wanted to be with me, but the rare times he was around me, I knew he was just making sure I was not up to no good.

I love to cook and spend quite a bit of time in the kitchen. Quincy took up his spot in the corner, right under foot. Precisely in front of a commonly used cabinet and where the refrigerator door would hit him if he did not move. But unless I left the kitchen he would not move. When I left the kitchen he was a crazy nervous wreck and would follow me everywhere; I could not even close the bathroom door. So I spent a lot of time in the kitchen over the next several weeks. I cleaned and organized every cabinet. I owe a lot of deep cleaning to Quincy that summer!

Slowly he got used to me being around and in his space. Slowly he would respond to me. Now please do not think respond meant that he looked at me and smiled a doggy smile or wagged a doggy tail. No, respond to me meant that he did not run away. It meant he would stay around, sit up and put

his head in the air and look away from me. This is dog language for, "I acknowledge you and I am not a threat to you." However, in people language this translated to, "You are lower than dirt and I need not even look at you or pay you any mind." My studying started to come in handy. I would get down near him and put my head up and turn my head away, essentially imitating his pose. We would hold this pose for some time. Then I would go to him, not looking at him and using my shoulder, touch him. Then I would back off and go away and clean another kitchen drawer.

After 2–3 weeks of this, he broke ranks and came to me! Gave me a sniff! It is hard to express how hard it was not to throw my arms around him and tell him, "good boy!" I would have to wait a long time for that to happen. I quietly celebrated with a glass of wine and bragging phone calls to my friends.

The thing is, though, I do not live alone! My loving husband was getting the doggy cold shoulder. The dog was totally freaked out when Kim would come inside. He would sit and just rock back and forth, as an autistic child will rock for comfort. He would hide behind furniture. He did not growl or stop me from going to Kim; we had just not better expect Quincy to do such a risky thing! Early on he had some nicknames that were more geared toward accuracy than were complimentary. Rescue Dog, POW (piece of work), WIP (work in progress), Houdini Dog and Schizo Dog were just a few of the repeatable ones. Please do not think us cruel. We were having a stressful time ourselves.

Since I was calling the vet's office so regularly they decided maybe he was a candidate for medication to help with the anxiety and stress. I am sure they would have medicated me too if their licensing went so far as to allow them to medicate the owners. They had to call Prozac in because I could not get Quincy into the car. I never ever thought I would have a dog on Prozac. This goes to show you can never predict the future. Also, you should never laugh at what other people do to (or *for*) their animals. I had to learn the hard way, so just take my word for it. Be understanding or you may be sent a challenge and have to eat your words.

We all survived that second weekend. We all had our various drugs started. We now had to figure out the second Monday. A friend loaned us a very nice large metal crate. Indy was very good at finding the treats inside, but Quincy would have none of it. He would go around the outside and manage to pull the treat to him. One time he went halfway in and got so nervous he forgot the treat when he quickly backed out. And do not let anyone tell you that dogs cannot walk backwards. If that dog wants to get away badly enough, he can go any direction possible. I left the crate up for almost a month. Put treats and pillows inside, did everything but go inside myself, not that I didn't consider doing that. But no dog went inside. So much for that. Another friend donated a beautiful outdoor doghouse. Quincy loved to hide behind it. But never, oh *never* did he go inside it.

So, Monday morning, I let Indy out. I let Quincy out. I left for work. Now, I was fairly certain he would be there upon my return. The question was would he come inside? Had he had enough of the woods the week before?

There he was, still on the property when I pulled up. Quincy actually seemed happy I was back. I went to the door. I unlocked the door. I called to him, did not look at him, stood out of the way, Indy went inside…and after a few moments of thinking, or simply gathering his courage, Quincy came inside for dinner.

Progress is measured in very small successes.

The Talking To

We carried on for a few weeks. Weeks of me
calling the vet's office daily. They were wonderful.
They gave me encouragement to carry on. After 5
weeks Quincy would come inside (*most of the time*) and
was starting to eat in the kitchen. Then I had a con-
ference to attend. I would be gone Thursday though
Sunday and since I was only 100 miles away, Kim
was to join me Saturday evening for dinner. We set
up for a dog sitter (female) and off I went. I talked
to Kim daily.

"How's Quincy?"

"Don't know."

"What do you mean you don't know?"

"He is back in the woods."

Oh, great. I called Kathy, the dog sitter,
Saturday evening, "Is Quincy there?"

"Right here," she replies. It appears that
Quincy will tolerate strange females, but not my
good, kind husband. Thank goodness it had not
been very cold or he may have really been harmed
living in the woods.

After that we went through a tough time for
almost 3 months. Quincy would not pee or poop on
the leash. So I tried to take him out every evening
at 8 p.m. I saw more starry nights that fall than
I had in years. I saw the northern lights! I froze,
got wet, and got snowed on because he would not
pee or poop if I did not escort him to his favorite
bathroom spot. Me, of course, ignoring any puppy

business. Then, it would be time to come inside. Sometimes Quincy would come in, other times, he would not. I would leave him out and come back in an hour to find him cowering at the door and ready to come inside. Kim could not let him inside or outside (or feed him or even *look* at him). Then one evening Quincy refused to come in. I went back down every hour, and, finally, at about 2 a.m. he came inside.

The next morning I was walking through the newly constructed sunroom and saw the patio storm door.

"Kim!" I cry out, "A bear tried to get inside last night."

"That was not a bear."

"Well it sure was not a raccoon. What could have twisted a sturdy metal door like that?"

Kim turned his gaze towards Quincy, who is of course hovering in the corner of the kitchen. The *DOG did that*? No Way. The metal storm door was a figure eight. How had he done that? Now, I think I am patient, but Kim is really patient. That is it; I am done, I am calling the local shelters. I did not want to send him on a 3-day trip south in November.

Kim said, "Give him another chance."

"No way."

Next day I call all the local shelters. The one person that would even talk to me said, after hearing the *why* of the call, "I do not want that dog."

"But why?" (*duh*).

"No one will want him. I will never get rid of him." I admit it, I pleaded with the woman.

"But some nice single retired lady would be great. He is really cute."

I got home that evening. Quincy was there, he came inside, and he ate in the kitchen and even took a treat. Then went to his corner. I went up to him, knelt down and actually looked at him. I pointed my finger at him, wagged it like an annoying mother, and said,

"You are one lucky dog. Kim is willing to give you one more chance. The local shelters do not even want you! You had better shape up or you are shipping south! And I mean it!"

He looked back at me, laid down in his corner with his head on his paws and sighed. I do not know if he understood the English or the finger wagging, but afterward things started, ever so subtly, to change. Oh, I still had to stand out in the rain and snow at night, and I still could not look at him, and Kim could not go near him, but somehow things started to change.

Talk and More Talk

If you have occasion to read pet training material, you will find a theme. Ignore the anxious dog. Do not say "poor baby" or feed into the anxiety, especially ill-placed anxiety. But after a few weeks it occurred to me that I was *always* ignoring him because he was *always* anxious. It was time to break the rules. Time to start talking. I was not sure if I should talk *to* him, since I could apparently be deadly and dangerous, so I just chattered.

I am not a natural chatterer. I found that it is really hard work to chatter. "...And now I am doing this and now I am doing that and the oven needs to be at..." and so forth. Also, the chattering had to be in happy voice. Let me tell you, if you have had a rotten day at work, coming home and saying in happy voice "I have had a *^&%(*!# day and everything went wrong and it rained and I forgot my umbrella and the zipper on my pants broke and ..." (*You get the idea.*) I know it is a scientific fact that if you smile your happy hormones go up, but if you really need to rant and you are doing it in a happy voice, it is singularly unsatisfying. It was working for Quincy. He would look up at me. He seemed calmer. He liked the happy chatter. So I kept talking to myself, hoping upon hope that someday I could talk to the dog.

I Never Walk Alone

I know that spiritually I am never alone, but now I am never alone in the physical world. I have a shadow everywhere I wander. And I mean *everywhere*. I want to make perfectly clear that I have never, not even once, considered dashing out the bathroom window. Yet my dog seemed to think this was an imminent possibility. In the hour before "The Walk" all my dogs have followed me into the bathroom, but Quincy took 18 months before he realized there was no other way out. Early on he would even peer around the shower curtain, "Are you still in there?" (an even harder escape than out the window).

I am followed up the stairs, down the stairs, picking vegetables in the garden, taking out compost, taking out trash, putting clothes on the line, and, of course, napping. Quincy learned "time for nap" very quickly. He also seemed to understand that that was quiet time. If someone drove by he would ever so softly jump and put his paws on the sill and peer out.

Please remember that if someone else were with me (i.e. Kim) Quincy would be behind a piece of furniture. We had made some progress, but... Even when he didn't need to hide behind furniture he still would hide behind his nice wood doghouse, never inside, always behind.

I spend a lot of time in the kitchen, thus so did Quincy. I suspected that soon he would be able to cook for me. I had to ask him to move constantly, "Quincy, excuse me." "Quincy, excuse me." "Quincy, sorry, excuse me." He would move from in front of the oven to in front of the sink to in front of the refrigerator to back in front of the oven. Sometimes, after an hour of this, he would actually move to the other side of the room. Then we both got to have some peace.

THE SKY IS FALLING

Quincy initially slept by the side of our bed but after a few weeks he had chosen a spot of his own. During our renovation, we had put in a dormer. The area next to the dormer had a low slung and deeply angled roofline. It makes a very cozy spot. The floor is heated so it is warm. It is somewhat cave-like so he feels safe from the back and can see all the deadly dangers coming towards him.

We usually have a lot of snow in the winter and we have a metal roof. This is very good because it means that Kim does not have to go up on the roof and rake the snow off. With a metal roof, the snow periodically falls off. Well, next to the dormer where Quincy slept the snow would build up then fall. One night in December, after a particularly large amount of snowfall, the roof let go a ton of snow. I was rudely awakened with a 60-pound quivering, anxious dog standing on my chest.

"What in the world?"

"Didn't you hear that?" Kim asked.

"What?"

"The snow that fell must have fallen from right under where Quincy lays. Sounded like the sky was falling."

"I did not hear it."

We tried for hours to calm down Quincy. I even got dressed and took him outside to prove to him the world had not ended. He was so distraught even Kim could touch him. To this day, when snow falls off the roof he jumps and gets a little nervous...

A Short Reprieve

A dear friend had died. I was in the living room crying. Quincy was behind a chair. Just before Kim came into the room to console me, I felt a wetness that was not my tears on my face. I turned and Quincy was touching my cheek with his nose. I smiled despite my grief. As Kim came in, Quincy returned to his spot behind the chair.

Quincy had reached out. He felt my sadness and was willing to overcome his fear for just a minute. I think I knew then that all would be well.

Gold, Silver and Bronze Treats

It was early January. Kim walked in the door one evening, home from work. I pronounced, "Kim you are now in charge of all that is good!" He slyly smiled and said, "I know." I did give him a big hug, but sadly had to bring him back down to earth.

"For the dog," I say.

"For the dog?" he asked.

"Yes, you are purveyor of gold treats."

"What ever are you talking about?"

Well I had been reading a lot of dog training and dog behavior books. One of them utilized a system of gold, silver and bronze treats. Kim was to be in charge of gold treats (hot dogs), and gold treats only. I was relegated to bronze (dry dog bone) and occasionally the rare silver (cheese stick).

For a month my poor husband would come in the door and I would have a bit of hot dog to hand him. He carried a hot dog around as much as he could. He would sit in a chair reading with one hand off the edge holding a hot dog. Indy loved it. Eventually, Quincy would come to Kim's hand and sniff. After 3 weeks, he took the piece of hot dog before rushing away. Kim still could not look at him or even talk to him. Quincy would cautiously slink to Kim's hand, take the hot dog, and rush back to hide behind a piece of furniture. I was thrilled. Kim and the dog had made contact. Kim kept at it. After a couple months, Quincy would be in his corner in the kitchen. When Kim came home, Kim would crouch down, look away or down, hold out his hand with a hot dog, and Quincy would carefully approach.

I had to train Kim as well as the dog. Kim had to learn how to be *little wolf*. Kim had to learn to greet Quincy as a little wolf. This is counter intuitive for humans want to stand up, put our arms out and cry out to the dog, "I am so happy to see you!" We had to engage Quincy dog style, not human style.

And then one evening in March, after 3 months of hot dog training, Quincy came to Kim, took the hot dog and stayed there. Kim cautiously left his hand there, yet did not try to touch him. Quincy, suddenly realizing he was close to scary man, rushed away. But by May Quincy would confidently come get his hot dog and stay a moment. Then one momentous day, Quincy let Kim touch him. Kim was looking away, reading, and trying to ignore Quincy, while actually gently scratching the dog behind one ear!

"Well," Kim said after Quincy had rushed off to hide, "I think he is becoming a WIP dog."

"What is a WIP dog?" I wanted to know.

Work In Progress. He had moved on from POW dog (Piece Of Work) to WIP dog (Work In Progress). We had hope.

Meanwhile, I am training Quincy to heel, come and stay. When he did these things I was allowed to dispense a piece of cheese stick. Since in the very beginning, he would not even take a treat, it was significant that he was even interested in them. He learned "heel" in 3 days. Even if he did not want

to heel, he would obey the command. One time we were walking by the neighbor's dog. Quincy and this dog were not the best of friends. So I put Quincy on heel. He ignored the dog and did a perfect heel. Then I released him. I tried to reward him with lots of praise and, of course, cheese, but he ignored me. He ignored me the whole way home. He even ignored me after the walk for a while. He would not take cheese and gave me a doggy cold shoulder. I had made him do something he did not want to do, and, like a petulant 3-year-old, Quincy was letting me know.

"Stay" was harder. He would stay if I was in front of him, but when I moved behind him, he was nervous and had to see me. Eventually, with me gently talking while he could not see me, he became reassured. While "stay" would continue to be hard if he could not tell where I was, he improved.

Every time Quincy came toward me outdoors, I said, "Come." Since he had already decided to come to me, I was not sure it was working. I always acted thrilled that he had come to me and rewarded him. Then one day, he took off, running across the field at full speed. He had spotted a deer and was on the chase. I yelled his name as loudly as I could and followed with a firm, "Come." On a dime, he turned and raced back to me as fast as he had run out.

"I think he has 'come' down," Kim said.

I gave Quincy a *whole* hot dog!

One last note on the gold and silver treats.

Try to remember to remove them from your pocket before doing laundry; while they do all right in the washing machine, it is not a happy time when they go though the dryer. Just thought I would share that advice.

It Takes a Village

We live on a dead end dirt road. There are two homes beyond ours and two below. It is about one mile up to our house from the main road. We have not traditionally tied our dogs. One, they are breeds that like to herd or guard so they do not tend to wander. Two, we have 50 acres of land and a large field for them to run around. Three, we have coyotes and I have always worried that a dog may need to defend itself. Fortunately the latter has never occurred. In the winter or inclement weather we leave the dogs inside when we are away from the house. But in the summer and on nice days they are outdoors. I come home at any time and there they are sitting on the porch or under the trees awaiting my arrival.

But one day Quincy got nervous and went down the road in the direction my car travels. Thankfully, the UPS man, who had met Quincy a few times and wooed the dog with treats, was turning into our road. He recognized Quincy and got out of the truck and told him to get on home. The UPS man then followed Quincy up the road to make sure he was home. We never heard again that he went traveling quite so far afield.

Our neighbors knew that we had a new and adjusting dog. They were helpful in training Quincy to stay off the road and reporting whenever he had lapses. When Quincy would forget to stay off the road I would retrain him. I took him to the road and in a deep voice tell him I did not like that. Then

I would put him up on the grass and in a happy voice say, "Good puppy." Three or four times I did this. He rarely goes into the road now even if something really interesting is out there. Without our neighbors and UPS man, Quincy would not have learned his boundaries.

THE GREAT OUTDOORS

In the first year of Quincy's living with us he did try to make new friends. The problem was he seemed to choose animals that, well, let us say were less than interested in receiving his attention. In the first few weeks of having him, I came home one day and getting him inside seemed easier then usual. He kept pawing at his face. What in the world have you gotten into? He let me come close and I touched his face and felt sharp pointy needles coming out of everywhere. Porcupine quills were all over his face. He was so unhappy about his fate that he was letting me inspect the situation.

This precipitated yet another call to the vet. "What do I do? Should I bring him to you?" The staff counseled me through my first quill removal surgery. I gathered up a good set of tweezers and got to work. Trying to get down as close as I could to the skin, I gently pulled quill after quill out. Quincy stood still and quiet, and never cried although it must have hurt. I murmured softly to him that he was very brave and a good boy. After some time at this I thought, "There, we are done!" Proud of myself I poured a glass of wine and got Quincy and Indy their dinner. But Quincy was not really interested in dinner. So I re-inspected him but could not find anything.

Fortunately, Kim came in the door. I relayed the situation to him and he murmured the appropriate condolences to Quincy, who at this point was too worried about his fate to run from Kim. We took the dog, leash, tweezers and each other into the laundry room, thinking there was less room for him to run off. I held Quincy and told him that everything would be OK and Kim did an inspection. Kim has had this happen to other dogs he has owned and thus expected what I did not; that Quincy's mouth or tongue was involved.

"Yep," Kim says "There is one in his gum and one in his tongue."

"Ouch! So what do we do?"

"We get them out of course."

"Of course" seemed easier said than done with a dog that will not even stay in the same room as you—and you are going to remove quills from his mouth?

"Well," Kim replies, "He is sitting in here with us now and not running off."

And so he was, looking very dejected, but not running off. So, we sat back down, I did the comforting and Kim did the de-quilling. When we were through Kim gave Quincy a good behind the ear scratch and told him he was very, very good. Finally we could all eat dinner.

The second animal that Quincy ran into, literally, was Tux. *Tux* is what I nickname the skunks that regularly visit our domain. Now this was late in the second fall we had Quincy, and not Quincy's fault. He had finally figured out to leave the porch and I could be inside and he would "Go Pee." This was a huge advance for him to go off and do his *stuff*!

One fine evening, Quincy headed around the corner of the house to his favorite spot and ran full speed right into Tux. Tux, being less than impressed by this interruption of his own ablutions did what skunks do when mad, sprayed. Hard. And close. That poor dog came running back inside to me so fast, his eyes tearing and crying, dripping with skunk juice. If he had not smelled so bad and so strong, and if he had not run inside the house it would have been funny. Quincy had me smelling like skunk. I was trying to get him back outside for a late night bath, but he was understandably anxious about the possibility of a reconnection with Tux.

46

"Kim" I yelled, "Help!"

"Whatever is the ma...oh man, he got it didn't he?"

"Quick get the dog shampoo and that de-skunk stuff someone gave us. Time to see if it works."

"Nothing is going to work with this. This is bad."

Poor Quincy kept rubbing his eyes and looking at me, as if to say, "Can't you fix it?" Outside, boots on, dog shampoo and de-skunk stuff at the ready, we bathed and bathed that dog like he had never been bathed before. We did not even have to leash him to keep him there. He just stood there reeking of skunk and looking like a wet rat. Anyone who thinks dogs have no sense of when they look and smell good and when they do not look and smell good has never had a dog badly skunked. Trust me, they know.

The great outdoors continued to impress Quincy. We had our first snow that year early December and it was a real snow. Not a dusting but a good few inches. I walked out onto the porch with him to look at the pretty morning. Quincy took one step down, then the second step down, and then looked at the sea of white. He put a paw out to touch the white sea and pulled back. I realized our Southern dog had never seen snow! Indy, who was born in Vermont in February, came out, ran off the porch into the sea of cloudy white stuff and peed.

"See," I said, "It is OK."

He turned to me. He turned to the snow. His bladder seemed to have entered into the conversation because he braved the last step. He took a few tentative steps before he fully believed this white cloud would hold him up and there was not some trick. I was laughing so hard my own bladder was talking. Whenever I laugh hard Quincy gets happy and secure. Thus encouraged (and filled with pee) he headed out to his bathroom area.

We had a lot of snow that season and Quincy loved the snow. During our walks, there is an area where he is allowed off the leash so he can run. He would run full speed down the snowmobile track and throw himself sideways into the snow bank. He would do this over and over in play. I would laugh and laugh. One of the funnier times he played in snow banks was when Kim was with us. Quincy ran full speed and jumped up on the high bank left by the plow, it held him up. He stood up there looking pleased as punch, so we obliged him and started laughing. Encouraged, he jumped down, ran across the road and jumped on the bank on the other side of the road. The trouble was this bank was softer and did not hold him. All we saw was dog tail. Now we were laughing so hard we couldn't walk. Quincy crawled out of the bank and shook himself off. He looked back at us, confirmed we had had our entertainment for the day and continued on his walk.

The second year we had Quincy and he would be near Kim, they went snowshoeing. On the way back Kim let him off the leash, Quincy was not *that* normal yet; he still needed the leash to be near Kim outside. They started down the hill to the house. Quincy was doing his normal run full speed ahead so as not to be too near Kim when he lost his footing, and in doing so completed a full somersault. Kim said it was so funny. Quincy's head went down and next thing they both knew Quincy had done a 360 degree turn in the air and landed on his feet. Since Kim was laughing, Quincy decided to do it again. I regret I did not see the dog somersault down the mountain. The next day though, while I was in the den doing my exercising I looked over at Quincy. He had his nose down on his dog bed and before I knew what was happening he did a somersault. After all, he just loves to practice new things.

LOVE ME TENDER DOG

We had Quincy for about a year when he wagged his tail the first time. Well, his tail doesn't wag. His tail whirls around. The first time we saw it I pointed and just started laughing at his whirling tail. Of course the more I laughed, the more it whirled. And whirled! We were thrilled that he was showing happiness.

Then a few weeks after that he was laying around, in front of the oven (*of course*) and rolled over onto his back exposing his abdomen. He wanted a belly rub! Although it took a year to want one, he decided that a good belly rub was very nice indeed and requests one frequently. He also is a party hound. For a dog so shy that he would hide behind furniture, he sure turned into a social butterfly! The first time I realized this was during a party for 40 guests that we threw for a friend. I was, where else, in the kitchen. I had not seen Quincy for a while but figured he was hiding up on his bed.

Kim came inside and said, "You will never believe it."

"What?" I said.

"Quincy is out there working the crowd."

"Our Quincy? Are you sure?" (Maybe someone had brought a look-alike?)

"Yup."

People later asked where the rescue dog was they had heard so much about. You know, the dog that hid behind the furniture? We proudly pointed to the social party animal.

While Quincy is not an in your face attention seeking dog, he loves loving. Anytime he senses someone may come down to his level and massage him and whisper sweet doggy nothings to him, he is ready. Amazingly, he has come to really love Kim's attentions. Kim massages him and gives him a nice rub down and Quincy would purr if he could, I just know it.

It had been a 2-year journey. Quincy went from being a dog who would not look at us, or be in the same room with Kim; escaping from the house and living in the woods; and we now have a great and loving friend. He is smart and he loves to be told that he's a good boy. Since he is always a good boy he is rewarded verbally many times a day!

His curiosity probably saved him, for he could never totally ignore us. That curious face would eventually peer around the kitchen island, a piece of furniture, a tree or his doghouse, as if to say, "And what are you doing now?"

EPILOGUE

"Kim, look at this face, he is so cute! Indy is really, really old and Quincy needs a playmate!"

"Oh my God!"

"Does this dog like men?"

At the vet's:

"Kim and I are considering another rescue dog to keep Quincy company. Indy is getting really old and cannot play any longer. What do you think?"

Long pause.

"Dr. DeFrahn, you and Kim have done a terrific job with Quincy but we cannot go through another rescue with you! Why don't you get a puppy the normal way?"

And so Etta , the *sub-standard* schnauzer puppy, joined the family.

To Say Nothing of the Dog

I did not start out wanting to be a rescue dog. It was not my fault that my beginnings were a bit rough. I never knew my parents. I was found as a wee barely born pup with my littermates in a dumpster behind a sandwich shop. I survived but my poor littermates did not. So from the beginning I was in full rescue mode. I did nothing bad or wrong to get there, it was my fate. Since you already know things have worked out extremely well for me, I guess I will not complain about my early days.

So for almost 2 years I was a southerner. They do things differently in the South, talk slower, move slower and eat differently. I have lots of fur and it was often hot there. My rescue *mom* took rescuing animals very seriously. You could say it was her mission. I had up to 50 other dogs to keep me company. Then she began to rescue big animals and she started giving up my friends for adoption. I was one of the last; I think I was a favorite of hers since she had to bottle-feed me in the beginning. I really liked my rescue mom and missed her a lot in my early time up north.

Now, the trip north was very long, a few years at least. I was in a van for a few days, then a bigger van for a few years then another car for another few days. My new mom, Linda, said it was 3 ½ days but I am quite sure it was much, much longer. Then when I FINALLY got out of a moving vehicle it was wet, cool and very, very different. There was a large man, my new mom and another dog and I was nervous. OK, I was *really* nervous. I think I may have snarled at Indy and I had to apologize for my initial rudeness, but Indy was a kind soul and forgave me readily. I made a vow to myself never to get into one of those moving things again. Regretfully I have had to be forced into one on occasion but I am sure to make my dislike of it felt by all involved.

My early days in the North were difficult. First, a man, Kim, lived there and I was frightened of him. Now I know he is good, but back then nothing was certain except the uncertainty of it all.

I had never seen these stair things. Stairs are very scary, especially going down. I had to be seriously encouraged (*OK dragged*) up and down stairs for a couple days. Once I was more confident I practiced the stairs. I am very physical and agile and I love to practice acts that have previously challenged me.

I had only been here 2 days when Linda went outside. She left me indoors. That was when I discovered that there are very few doors that will contain me. I just pushed and I was outside! I was not sure what to do and could not see Linda. So I thought I would take a stroll. I got a bit disoriented and while I was scared of Linda I was glad she came along and found me. Funny thing though, she sat on the ground and started chatting to trees! I had never seen a human engaged in such absurd behavior so I thought I should go over and see if she was all right. I guess she just likes to chat to trees because she seemed fine. She attached me to the walking rope and put me in the dreaded car and we went back up the hill.

Then after a few days they left and locked me inside! I admit it, I freaked out! I am ashamed to admit this, I even left a doggy poop inside and I never do that! I crashed around the house looking for an escape. I tore up a couple rooms with windows that looked like viable escape routes but they did not pan out. Then I turned a door handle and was free. Yet another door that could not contain me! (Getting back inside doors was more difficult and took me time to perfect.) Free to do what? I was far away from home, scared, and regretfully, I had left my food inside, so I was hungry after all my indoor activity.

When Linda came home she seemed stressed to see me outdoors. She tried to put me on the walking rope but I was too quick. I am very quick when I need to be. I ran and hid in some trees. She drove all around and I could hear her calling to me from my little spot in the woods but I decided to case this joint out some more before I returned. I wanted to observe the new pack before I was comfortable enough to go inside. Wouldn't you want to check out new pack mates that talked to trees? I needed to observe this new pack to see if there was any other strange behavior. I can tell you though, I had a rough few nights in the woods with all that rain. I don't think it stopped raining for weeks.

Anyway, one day I was at the edge of the woods watching the new pack. Linda and Indy came out and started to play. This was at least normal pack behavior. I was so lonely I ran over and wanted to be one of them. For a second I forgot I was casing the place and just wanted to be a dog getting attention. Linda took advantage of my being so close and put me on the walking rope. Although I was unhappy about it at the time, it was probably a good thing. The woods were not getting any warmer or drier.

It is a very good thing that I can hold my urine and poopies for a very long time because I simply do not appreciate doing these personal things while on a leash or being observed. I am very reserved. I do not think that I am unusual in this regard. Also, while performing these acts of a personal nature, a dog is vulnerable. But it did cause some occasional difficulties and certainly consternation on Linda's part.

In the beginning I had to keep Linda in sight. She spent a lot of time in the room she calls a kitchen; it usually smells fabulous. I found a safe corner in the kitchen where it was warm and dry and I could keep a good eye on everything. Apparently I was often in the way in this corner and Linda would say, "Excuse me, Mr. Quincy," and I would have to move out of the way. Of course I would wait just a few seconds and then quickly assume my spot again.

Linda did her very best to be a good dog. She crawled around on the floor and attempted to engage me in nonthreatening dog behavior. In reality however, Linda is not a very good dog. She did not, *nor does she now*, like to have her butt sniffed. Further proof that she isn't a very good dog—she never tried to sniff my butt. I tried many times to teach her, but she is not as trainable as I am, and she never learned the *butt hello*.

My first few months with Linda and Kim were very quiet months. Linda did not talk much to me and Linda and Kim seemed to be quiet people. I do admit I thought I had been a bad puppy because I was used to being talked to. I even wondered if Linda had hurt her voice talking to the trees. Then one day Linda started chattering, and chattering, and chattering. She always chattered in a nice low, calm, lilting tone and this made me very happy. I felt that I was a good puppy and I was being told on a regular basis how good I was being. I was also being told how handsome I was. I was pleased someone finally noticed! I must admit there was the occasional time when Linda was chattering and I felt her happiness was less than sincere. After all, I am a dog and we are very sensitive to our packmate's feelings. In fact there was a time that Linda had water on her face and seemed very, very sad so I went to her and gave her a quick lick on the cheek to let her know I cared.

Getting used to Kim was quite a trial for me and I suspect a trial for Kim also. Kim never said a bad word to me or raised his voice to me. But he was a man and he was big and he was scary. I tried my best to keep a good distance from him. In this kitchen room there was a long thing in the middle of the floor, an *eye land* they called it. Well it was very convenient to keep away from Kim, any time he moved from his end, I moved from my end. Around and around we'd go. Best always to keep something solid between me and the dangerous guy.

He developed a curious habit of walking around the house holding bits of hot dog. I had never seen such a thing before. Eventually I decided if he was going to walk around with a hot dog in his hand and not eat such a delicious treat, well, I was just going to have to eat it for him. Now, if I had a hot dog and Indy had come up to me and wanted it, I admit that I would not have shared my hot dog. But when I went to Kim and took his hot dog from him, he seemed ecstatic. Humans are just weird about hot dogs and other good things to eat, at least these humans. They also have the same reaction with cheese sticks. They carry around cheese sticks, yet they do not gobble them right up. I am happy to help them get rid of their hot dogs and cheese sticks particularly as it makes them very happy when I do so.

The North has interesting creatures. Two I especially recall, and not at all fondly. One was a prickly fellow that tricked me into trying to share a good butt sniff and then attacked me from the rear. I had spears in my face, my mouth, my gums even in my tongue and it really hurt. Fortunately, Kim and Linda helped me with that situation.

The other creature I did not like meeting was one they call *Tux*. I had finally become confident enough to go out to my favorite bathroom site. I ran full speed to go around the house to my spot. I rounded the corner and bumped full force into a black thing with a white stripe. I tried to apologize for my invading the creature's bathroom time, being shy about that myself, but before the words were out of my mouth it sprayed me with a terrible stench. I was dripping with it and ran to Linda and Kim for help. I was very embarrassed to smell so bad. I am quite vain about my hygiene.

When I had been in the North for about 5 months, something very curious occurred. I got up, went outside and while I was sleeping, the world had gone white. There were clouds on the ground. They did not appear sturdy to me, so I stopped in full brake mode. I watched as Indy nonchalantly carried on as if nothing was abnormal. I cried to her, "Watch out, the clouds will not hold you!" But she was very deaf by that time and she couldn't hear me. What a surprise I got when the clouds held her up! So I cautiously tried it myself. Linda was telling me it was OK. "It is called 'snow,' Quincy." So I very bravely went off the porch, one paw at a time. And lo and behold, the snow held me up! Since then, I think snow is grand fun. You can run and throw yourself into it and not get hurt. You can even do somersaults in the snow. If you can perfect the somersaults you will make humans laugh. They are easily entertained.

Here is another interesting thing about these packmates. When they go away, even if they are only gone a very short time, upon their return they act so happy to see me! I decided the best course of action was to act just as excited to see them. They seem to appreciate it, plus it can get you a treat.

Excuse me I think I hear a car.

...

False alarm

As I was saying:

In my first year I was very anxious. I felt I had to hide behind furniture and in corners. I had to follow Linda everywhere. She would go into a small room every day so I would follow her. She got into a rain box everyday so I would make sure she was safe in there. I followed her everywhere. She did not seem to mind and it made me feel better to have her in sight. The only place I would not, *nor will I* follow her, is into the car.

They got me a nice large doghouse. Regretfully, I did not take to being inside the doghouse. I did love hiding behind the doghouse. I could hide in between the doghouse and the big house. This was very safe and had an excellent quick escape route.

When I was not in my corner in the kitchen, I was on my dog bed under an eave. The floor was warm. I had a wall to my back and an easy escape from the front. One night while I was resting nicely in the quiet hours, all of a sudden the sky fell. It made a terrible racket. I quickly ran to the packmates to warn them of impending doom. I jumped up on their bed and stood over them and tried my best to tell them the sky was falling. Yet they seemed unfazed. I spent the next few hours trying to tell them to escape, but they would not leave. Eventually, I got really tired from all the excitement and tried to rest myself. To this day when I hear the sky fall, I get scared. Linda tries to softly tell me it is OK, but a dog never knows.

I am not sure why I was so anxious. Nothing bad was being said to me, nor was I being harmed. The food was good and there were all those hot dog and cheese stick bits, so I was being well fed. I may have a wee bit of autism. Who knows? I heard from the talking box that it is being over diagnosed, so I am not sure. I seem to love routine more than other dogs I have encountered. While they like routine, they also love the surprise car ride, swim, and change in their day. Not me. As I have gotten older, I have decided to just love myself as I am. Linda and Kim love me, so it cannot be all bad.

I hear another car.

I am pleased to say this time it is Linda's car. I must go now. I am ready for a nice belly rub and some dinner. It has been delightful chatting with you and I wish you the very best.

BOOKS OF REFERENCE

The Loved Dog by Tamar Geller, published by Simon Spotlight Entertainment, 2007.

This book has a lot of great training ideas, including the gold, silver and bronze treat idea.

Inside of a Dog by Alexander Horowitz, published by Scribner, 2009.

How to Speak Dog by Stanley Coren, published by Fireside, 2000.